TREETOPS CLASS

STORIES OF
SHERLOCK HOLMES

ARTHUR CONAN DOYLE
adapted by Trevor Millum

OXFORD
UNIVERSITY PRESS

OXFORD
UNIVERSITY PRESS

Great Clarendon Street, Oxford OX2 6DP

Oxford University Press is a department of the University of Oxford.
It furthers the University's objective of excellence in research, scholarship,
and education by publishing worldwide in

Oxford   New York

Auckland   Bangkok   Buenos Aires   Cape Town   Chennai
Dar es Salaam   Delhi   Hong Kong   Istanbul   Karachi   Kolkata
Kuala Lumpur   Madrid   Melbourne   Mexico City   Mumbai   Nairobi
São Paulo   Shanghai   Singapore   Taipei   Tokyo   Toronto

with an associated company in Berlin

Oxford is a registered trade mark of Oxford University Press
in the UK and in certain other countries

ISBN 0 19 919327 4

Cover: David Axtell
Inside Illustrations: Shirley Bellwood

Printed in Great Britain

About the Author

ARTHUR CONAN DOYLE

1859–1930

Arthur Conan Doyle was trained as a doctor, but wanted to be a writer. He wrote his first Sherlock Holmes story in 1887, and it was a huge success. His readers demanded more stories.

By 1893, the writer had decided that he didn't want to be known only as 'the Holmes man'. So he wrote a story in which Holmes died. When it was published, some people in London wore black clothes, as if a relative of theirs had died! And they never stopped asking for more Holmes stories, so Conan Doyle had to bring his detective back to life.

The Boscombe Valley Mystery

CHAPTER I

An Ordinary Crime?

My name is Dr Watson and I have the good fortune to be the friend and companion of Sherlock Holmes. I try to keep a record of the cases he has solved. I have been with him many times when he has solved cases with just a few clues and his powerful brain.

One such case was the Boscombe Valley Mystery. I knew nothing about it until I got a telegram early one morning at home. It was from Holmes, asking me to go with him to the West of England. My wants are few and simple so I very swiftly packed a case, said farewell to my wife and was at Paddington in less than an hour.

Holmes was pacing up and down the platform. He was instantly recognizable: tall and gaunt – and dressed in his long grey cloak and deerstalker hat. 'It is really very good of you to come, Watson. I need someone I can rely on.'

We had the carriage to ourselves and Holmes spent the time reading through a huge pile of newspapers. Now and then he stopped to make notes and to think. Finally, he rolled the papers into a ball and threw them onto the luggage rack.

'Have you heard anything of the case?' he asked.

'Not a word. I've not seen a paper for days.'

'Hmm,' said Holmes. 'It's one of those simple cases which are so extremely difficult.'

'What do you mean?'

'The more ordinary a crime seems to be, the more difficult it is to see the solution. It is the unusual which makes things easy!'

'What kind of crime are we dealing with?'

'Murder, Watson. A serious case has already been made against the son of the murdered man. It happened in Boscombe Valley, near Hereford. The owner of much land in that area is a Mr John Turner. He came back from Australia a few years ago and settled here.'

'Made his fortune, did he?'

'Enough to buy several farms. One he let out to another Australian, Mr Charles McCarthy. McCarthy has a son of eighteen, called James.'

'Are there no wives?' I asked.

'Neither of the wives is still living, but Turner has one daughter of similar age to James.'

'And the murder?'

'It seems that last Monday, McCarthy left his house at Hatherley at about three in the afternoon. He walked down to Boscombe Pool, a small lake at the end of

Boscombe Valley. He told his servant that he had an appointment at three o'clock. He never came back alive.

'McCarthy was seen walking towards the pool by two people. Both say he was walking alone. The gamekeeper also says that a few minutes later James McCarthy went the same way, carrying a gun. He thought the son was following his father.'

'And was the father shot?' I asked.

'Oh no,' replied Holmes. 'Please wait. There was another witness. Patience Moran, daughter of the lodge-keeper on the Boscombe Estate, was picking flowers in the woods. She says that she saw James and his father having a violent quarrel. She heard Charles McCarthy using strong language to his son and she saw the son raise his hand as if to strike his father.'

Holmes continued, 'She ran away and told her mother. Almost as soon as she had finished telling her story, James McCarthy ran up and said he had found his father dead. They followed him and found the body by the side of the pool. The head had been beaten in by blows from some heavy and blunt weapon.'

'Such as the butt-end of a gun?' I asked.

'Exactly. Anyway, Watson, James McCarthy has been arrested and charged with his father's murder. It looks exceedingly grave against the young man.'

'Has he said anything?'

'Indeed he has. And it makes an interesting case.

According to James McCarthy, he had been away in Bristol for three days. He came back to find his father out. He set out to do some rabbit shooting at the other side of Boscombe Pool. About a hundred yards from the pool he heard a cry of "Cooee!" which was the usual signal between him and his father.

'His father was surprised to see him. For some reason, an argument took place and James walked off.

He had not gone far when he heard a dreadful cry.

'According to his story, he returned and found his

father dying. He held him in his arms but he could do nothing. He then ran off to the lodge-keeper's for help.'

'Is there nothing else to go on?' I asked.

'Two things which may turn out to be important,' said Holmes. 'James heard his father speak before he died. He said he spoke about a rat.'

'A rat!'

'Precisely, my dear Watson. And the other matter was the subject of the quarrel.'

'Which was?'

'James McCarthy refused to tell the coroner what they quarrelled about.'

'Refused?'

'Quite so.' Holmes looked up at me, raised his eyebrows and smiled. 'You see why I am interested, Watson. This is not such a simple case as they would have us believe.'

CHAPTER 2

A Blow from Behind

We arrived at the Hereford Arms in Ross at half past four. We were sipping our tea when the door burst open and in rushed one of the loveliest young women I have ever seen.

'Oh, Mr Sherlock Holmes!' she cried. 'I am so glad you have come. I know that James didn't do it. We have known each other since we were children. He is too tender-hearted to hurt a fly.'

'You may rely on my doing all that I can,' replied Holmes, deducing correctly that the lady was Mr Turner's daughter, Alice.

'James never did it,' she repeated. 'And about his quarrel with his father – I am sure he refused to speak of it because it concerned me.'

'In what way?'

'Mr McCarthy wanted James to marry me. We have always loved one another like brother and sister – but James is so young – and he is not willing to commit himself to such a step . . .' She blushed and I deduced that she would not object to marrying him, however.

'Thank you,' said Holmes. 'And may I see your father tomorrow?'

'I am afraid the doctor won't allow it.'

'The doctor?'

'Have you not heard? Poor Father has not been strong for years but this has made him quite ill. He was such a strong man once – when he was in Australia. Mr McCarthy was the only man who knew him in those days.'

'Really?' said Holmes. 'That is interesting. Thank you, Miss Turner, you have been a great help.'

She smiled gratefully at him. 'I must go home now. Father misses me so, if I leave him.' She hurried from the room as impulsively as she had entered.

Holmes decided to set off for Hereford immediately to see James McCarthy, and while he was away I pondered the details of the murder. The local paper had the full inquest report which included the surgeon's description of the injuries. The bones on the left hand side of the skull, at the back, had been shattered by a heavy blow.

This gave me pause for thought. Such a blow must have been struck from behind, which is not what you would expect in a face-to-face argument. Then there was the matter of the man's dying words. 'A rat...' What could it mean?

Holmes returned late without much more information. He had found out, though, the truth about James' feelings towards Miss Turner. 'He is madly in love with her,' remarked Holmes.

'Then why argue with his father about the match?'

'Because, Watson, he is already married.'

'Great heavens, Holmes! He is hardly more than a boy!'

'And he was even more of a boy when he got himself into the clutches of a barmaid in Bristol. He married her secretly over a year ago when Miss Turner was away at boarding school.'

'So he is being scolded for not doing what he would love to do! How maddening!'

'Quite so. However, good may come of this evil. It seems that the barmaid found out he was in serious trouble. She has thrown him over. She has written to

say that she has a husband already in the Bermuda Dockyard!'

'So there is no tie between them?'

'Happily so – but a small comfort for being in prison on a murder charge.'

'But if he is innocent, who has done it?'

'Let me draw your attention to two things, Watson. First, the murdered man had an appointment with someone. That person could not have been his son. His son was away and he didn't know when he was returning.'

'Of course. And the second thing?'

'The murdered man was heard to cry "Cooee!" before he knew his son was anywhere near. The case depends upon such things!'

Holmes closed his eyes and would say no more.

CHAPTER 3

The Scene of the Crime

The following morning we set off for Hatherley Farm and the Boscombe Pool. As the carriage bounced down the country lanes, Holmes turned to me.

'One other interesting fact, Watson. Mr McCarthy lived at Hatherley Farm rent free.'

'How very generous of Mr Turner,' I replied. 'But then, they were friends from Australia.'

'Does it not seem odd, though? McCarthy, who had so little of his own, talked of marrying his son to Turner's daughter. He talked of it in a very confident way – but I have discovered that Turner himself was against it.'

It did seem odd but I could deduce nothing from it. We soon arrived at the farm, a comfortable-looking two-storey building. The maid, at Holmes' request, showed us the boots McCarthy had been wearing. She also found a pair of his son's boots.

Holmes measured them all very carefully and then set off to the pool. It was damp marshy ground and there were marks of many feet on the path and on the short grass beside it. 'How simple it would have been,' exclaimed Holmes, 'if I had been here before they came like a herd of buffalo. Many of the important tracks have been obscured.'

He peered at the ground, then cried, 'Aha! Here are three separate tracks of the same feet.'

He took out a lens and lay down to get a better view, all of the time talking to himself. 'These are young McCarthy's feet. Twice he was walking and once he ran swiftly. The soles are deeply marked but the heels hardly visible. That bears out his story. Here are the father's feet as he paced up and down. Ha! What have we here? Tip-toes. Tip-toes! Square, too. Quite unusual boots. Now, where did they come from?'

Holmes paced up and down, sometimes losing and sometimes finding the track. He stopped in the edge of the wood and under the shadow of a great beech tree he lay down again. He stayed there a long time, turning over leaves and dry twigs. A jagged stone was lying among the moss; he picked it up and examined it carefully. Then he got up and followed a pathway through the woods which led to the main road, where he stopped.

He showed me the stone. 'This may interest you,' he said. 'If I am not mistaken, the murder was done with it.'

He did not sound as if he expected to be mistaken but I had to ask, 'How can you tell? There are no marks on it.'

'The grass was growing under it so it had only been there a few days. It matches the injuries and there is no sign of another weapon.'

'And the murderer?'

'The murderer is a tall man, left-handed. He limps with the right leg and wears thick-soled shooting boots. He smokes Indian cigars, uses a cigar holder and carries a blunt penknife. There are several other indications, but these may be enough to aid us in our search.'

Holmes was silent for a long time and we did not speak again until we were back at the Hereford Arms.

CHAPTER 4

A Rat!

After lunch, Holmes sat with his tapering fingers together, staring into space. Then he turned to me.

'I don't know quite what to do, Watson. I should value your advice. Let me explain.'

'Pray do so.'

'Let us presume that what young James said was true.'

'In what respect?'

'About two things in particular. One I mentioned earlier – that his father called "Cooee" *before* seeing him. The other was McCarthy's dying words about a rat.'

'What of this Cooee, then?'

'It could not have been meant for his son. As far as McCarthy knew, his son was in Bristol. The Cooee was meant to call the person he was meeting. But Cooee is an Australian greeting. Hence he was expecting to meet someone from Australia.'

I nodded. 'And the rat?'

Holmes took out a folded paper from his pocket. 'This is a map of the colony of Victoria in Australia. I had it sent over this morning.' He put his hand over part of the map. 'What do you read?'

'ARAT,' I said.

'And now?' He raised his hand. I could see the whole word. 'BALLARAT.'

'Quite so. That was the word that McCarthy spoke. His son heard the last part only. He was trying to say the name of his murderer. "So-and-so of Ballarat." '

'That's wonderful!'

'It's obvious. Now, you see, I have narrowed down the field. A tall Australian who is at home in the district. At home enough to find his way through the back of the estate.'

'His height you deduced from the length of his stride – and his boots. But what about his lameness?'

'The mark of his right foot was always less clear than his left. He put less weight on it. Why? Because he limped.'

'But his left-handedness?'

'You noticed the injury as reported at the inquest. A blow struck from behind yet from the left side. Surely a left-handed man? He stood behind the tree during the argument between James and his father. He even smoked there – I found the ash of a cigar. As you know, I am an expert on tobacco ash. I then discovered the cigar stump in the moss where he had thrown it.'

'And the cigar holder?'

'The cigar had not been in his mouth, therefore he had used a holder. The tip had been cut off, not bitten. It was not a clean cut – so I deduced a blunt penknife.'

'I see where this all points. The murderer must be – '

'Mr John Turner!' cried a voice. It was the hotel waiter, opening the door. He showed a visitor into the room.

The man who entered was a strange and impressive figure.

He had a slow limping step but his craggy face and huge arms and legs gave an impression of strength of body and character. His face was white and his lips tinged with blue. As a doctor I could see that he was a very ill man.

'Pray take a seat,' said Holmes. 'You got my note?'

'The lodge-keeper brought it. You said you wished to see me here to avoid scandal.'

'I thought people would talk if I came to the Hall.'

'And why did you wish to see me?' the man asked, wearily.

'I know all about McCarthy,' said Holmes.

The old man sunk his face in his hands. 'God help me!' he cried. 'But I would have spoken out. I would not have let that young man come to harm.'

'I am glad to hear it,' said Holmes gravely.

'I would have spoken of it already. But my dear daughter: it will break her heart when she sees me arrested.'

'It may not come to that,' said Holmes.

'What?'

'I am no police officer. Your daughter invited me here and I am acting in her interests. Young McCarthy must be got off, however.'

'I am a dying man,' said Turner. 'The doctor says I have but a month. Yet I would sooner die under my own roof than in jail.'

'Just tell us the truth while I jot down the facts. You will sign it with Watson as witness. If the case goes against young McCarthy I shall use your confession. You may be assured I shall not use it unless it is absolutely needed.'

'It's as well,' said the old man. 'I doubt I shall live until the trial. But I would still like to spare Alice the shock. I will tell you all. It will not take long.'

CHAPTER 5

A Riddle Answered

'This man McCarthy was a devil. His grip has been upon me these twenty years. He has blasted my life.

'It began in the sixties at the gold diggings. I was young and hot-blooded but I had no luck with my search for gold. I took to drink and made bad friends. I became a highway robber. There were six of us and we had a wild free life. Black Jack of Ballarat was the name I took.

'One day a gold convoy came from Ballarat to Melbourne. We attacked it and in the fight three of our boys were killed before we got the swag. I put my pistol to the head of the driver – it was this man McCarthy. I wish to the Lord I had shot him then...

'We got away with the gold and became wealthy men. Later, I made my way to England. I wanted to settle down and do some good with my money, to make up for the way I had earned it. I married and, though my wife died young, she left me my darling daughter Alice.

'I did my best to lead a good life and to make up for my past. All was going well until McCarthy laid his grip upon me!

'I had gone to London on business. There in Regent Street I met him. He had hardly a coat on his back or a boot to his foot.

' "Well, here we are, Jack!" he said. "We'll be as good as family to you, me and my son. You can have the keeping of us. And if you don't, it's a fine law-abiding country – and there's always the police . . ."

'Well, they came down here and there was no shaking them off. They lived rent free at Hatherley on my best land. There was no rest. No peace. No forgetfulness. Turn where I would, there was his cunning, grinning face at my elbow. It grew worse as Alice grew up. He saw that I was more afraid of her knowing my past than I was about the police. Whatever he wanted, I gave without question. Land, money, houses – until at last he asked what I could not give. He asked for Alice.

'His son had grown up. It seemed a great stroke to him to marry his son to my girl. I was ill and when I died his family would take the whole property.

'But I was firm. I would not do it. I did not dislike the lad but the McCarthy blood was in him and that was enough. McCarthy threatened me. I braved him to do his worst. Finally, we were to meet at the pool midway between our houses to talk it out.

'I went down there and heard him talking with his son. I smoked a cigar and waited in the trees till he was alone. But as I listened, all that was dark and bitter in me seemed to come uppermost. He was urging his son to marry Alice with no regard for what she might feel. It drove me mad to think that I and all that I held most dear should be in the power of such a man! I had to silence his foul tongue! I did it, Mr Holmes. I struck him down like a venomous beast. That is the truth, gentlemen, of what occurred.'

'It is not for me to judge you,' said Holmes as Turner signed the statement. 'You know that you are to answer for your deeds at a higher court than ours.'

'Farewell, then,' said the old man. 'Your own death-beds, when they come, will be the easier for the thought of the peace which you have given to mine.' He stumbled slowly from the room.

'God help us,' said Holmes after a long silence. 'Why does fate play such tricks with poor helpless worms?'

James McCarthy was acquitted at the trial, mainly because of the evidence presented by Holmes to the Defence. Old Turner lived another seven months. There is now every chance that James and Alice may yet live happily together – in ignorance of the cloud which rests upon their past.

The Adventure of the Blue Carbuncle

CHAPTER I

A Goose and a Bowler Hat

I called on my friend Sherlock Holmes soon after Christmas. He greeted me warmly and we sat by his cheery fire. It was frosty outside and I was glad of the warmth. As we sat down, he pointed to an old bowler hat.

'An interesting trophy, Watson.'

'To you, Holmes, I am sure it is.'

'It was found by Peterson, the commissionaire.'

I knew Peterson. He wore an official uniform and acted as doorkeeper for the block of apartments in which Holmes lived.

Holmes went on, 'Peterson was going home late one night when he noticed a tall man in front of him, carrying a goose – no doubt for the Christmas meal. As he reached the corner of Goodge Street, he bumped into some rough types coming in the opposite direction. They were drunk and for some reason a fight looked about to start. The man raised his walking stick to defend himself and smashed a pane of glass behind him.

'At this point Peterson came along and the roughs ran off. In the dark his uniform probably made him look like a policeman. The tall man ran off too, perhaps thinking that he would be in trouble for breaking the window. Anyway, in the upset he left behind the goose and the hat, which Peterson brought to me. He knows how I like even a small mystery.'

'So the poor fellow lost his Christmas dinner!'

'It would seem so. Inside the hat there was a label, with the name "Mr Henry Baker" – but there are hundreds of people with that name in London. I told Peterson to take the goose himself but I retained the hat.' Holmes offered it to me. 'See what you can deduce from it,' he said.

I looked at the battered object. The red silk lining was now dirty and though holes had been made for a hat securer, the elastic was missing. The hat was very dusty and there were patches where the black had faded. Some of these had been smeared with ink.

'I can deduce nothing,' I said.

Holmes took the hat and gazed at it in the peculiar fashion which I had seen so many times before. He then said, 'The owner used to be well-off, but is no more. He used to think ahead but is now more careless. He is not very fit, probably middle-aged, and his house does not have gas. Oh, and he has grey hair, recently cut, on which he puts lime-cream. I doubt that his wife cares for him as much as she used to.'

'Heavens, Holmes, how can you know all that?' I cried.

'This hat is three years old; these flat brims slightly curled were in fashion then. It is of good quality – look at the lining. So, he bought an expensive hat three years ago but now it is old.'

'But he still wears it,' I said.

'Exactly. So perhaps he has fallen on hard times. He used to take more care than he does now. See the marks for the hat-securer – the elastic is now broken and he has not replaced it. He has become careless. However, the ink marks show that he still makes some effort as he is trying to hide the fade marks on the outside.'

'And the other details?' I asked.

'If you look closely you will see the small grey hair ends showing a recent haircut; and you will catch the smell of lime-cream. There are marks of moisture – almost certainly sweat. I deduce that someone who perspires so much is not fit.'

'But his wife . . . You said – '

'Ah, yes. Just a guess, Watson. The hat has not been brushed for weeks. What loving wife would allow her husband to go out like that? When I see you in such a hat I shall know that your wife no longer cares for you!'

I smiled. 'Well, perhaps. But what about the gas – or lack of it?'

'There are a number of tallow stains on the hat. This chap uses candles rather than gaslight.'

I was amused by Holmes' deductions. 'Very interesting, Holmes. What a pity no crime has been committed.'

As if on cue, the door burst open. It was Peterson.

'Mr Holmes! The goose, sir!' he gasped.

'Has it come to life and flown away?' asked Holmes.

'See here, sir. See what my wife found in its crop.' He held out his hand. There in his palm was a jewel, a blue stone that shone like a little light.

'By Jove!' exclaimed Holmes. 'It is the blue carbuncle!'

'Not the Countess of Morcar's jewel?' I cried. 'The one stolen from the Hotel Cosmopolitan?'

'Exactly that,' said Holmes. 'Just a few days ago. John Horner, a plumber, is accused of the crime.' He picked up a newspaper and shortly found what he was seeking.

'According to the news reports, Horner was asked to come and do some minor work in the Countess of Morcar's dressing room. James Ryder, a porter, brought him to the room to do the work but was then called away for a while. When he came back he found that the bureau had been forced. The jewel-case was open and it was empty. Ryder gave the alarm and that evening Horner was arrested.'

'What did he have to say?' I asked.

'He said he was innocent. However, he has a previous conviction for robbery and he will stand trial next month. The jewel, however, was not found . . . '

'Until now!'

'Indeed, Watson. Now let us think how far we have got with this little mystery. Here is the jewel. The jewel came from the goose and the goose came from a Mr Henry Baker. So we must find Mr Baker, the owner of the hat!'

I nodded.

'The easiest way may be to place an advertisement.' He turned to Peterson. 'I wonder if you would be so kind . . . ' Holmes spent a few moments drafting a short advert. 'This will do. "Found at the corner of Goodge Street, a goose and a black bowler hat. Mr Henry Baker may have both by applying at 6.30 tomorrow at 221B Baker Street.'''

CHAPTER 2

Mr Baker Arrives

The advert was placed in several evening papers. Peterson also purchased a goose, similar to the one he and his family had eaten. Just before 6.30 the next day I went to join Holmes and we waited to see if the owner of the goose would turn up.

At 6.35 there was a knock at the door. A tall man stood there, dressed in a black frock coat which had seen better days.

'Mr Henry Baker, I believe,' said Holmes. 'I think this might be yours.' He pointed to the hat.

'Yes, sir. That is my hat without a doubt.'

'Good. The goose, I'm afraid, we had to eat,' said Holmes, smiling.

'You've eaten it!' exclaimed the man.

'It would have gone bad,' said Holmes. 'But this other one – ' he pointed to the table – 'is the same size and is much fresher. Will that not suit you?'

'Oh, yes,' said Mr Baker, with relief. 'It will suit us very well.'

'We still have the feathers, the legs, the crop and so on of your own bird if you wish to have them . . .'

The man laughed. 'I have no use for such things,' he said.

'Very well,' said Holmes. 'But could you tell me where you got the bird? It was a fine one.'

'Of course. At the Alpha Inn, near the Museum. We pay a few pence each week through the year for our Christmas goose. The landlord buys the birds at a good rate and we take them home on Christmas Eve.'

With a few more polite words, the man bowed to us both, thanked us again and left with his hat on his head and the goose under his arm.

'So much for Mr Henry Baker,' said Holmes. 'But I think we might visit the landlord of the Alpha Inn. Would you like a glass of beer, Watson?'

CHAPTER 3

A Goose Chase

In fifteen minutes we were at the Alpha Inn, a small public house in Bloomsbury. Holmes pushed open the door of the saloon bar and ordered two glasses of beer from the ruddy-faced, white-aproned landlord.

'Is your beer as good as your geese?' he asked.

The landlord looked surprised. 'My geese?' he exclaimed.

'Yes. I was speaking only half an hour ago to a Mr Henry Baker. He was one of your goose club members.'

'Ah, I see. But them is not our geese. I gets 'em from the market in Covent Garden.'

Holmes nodded. 'I see. Who is your man there?'

'I always goes to Breckinridge. Would you be thinking of joining the goose club, sir?'

'Thank you, no,' said Holmes. He sipped the beer appreciatively. 'Your good health, landlord.'

We drank our beer and set out once again. This time we walked south and at last came to Covent Garden Market. One of the largest stalls had the name 'Breckinridge' on it. Holmes walked up to a horsey-faced man with trim side-whiskers who seemed to be the owner.

'Sold out of geese, I see,' said Holmes.

'You can get some from over there,' the man replied, pointing to another stall.

'I was told you sold the best.'

'Who by?'

'The landlord of the Alpha.'

'I sent him two dozen, it's true.'

'And where did you get them from?' asked Holmes.

To our surprise the question seemed to anger the man.

'Now then, mister,' he said with his hands on his hips. 'What are you getting at? Let's have it straight.'

'It is straight enough. I should like to know who sold you the geese which you sold to the Alpha.'

'Well, I shan't tell you.'

Holmes sighed, as if the matter was not important. 'I wonder that you should be upset over such a small thing.'

'Upset! You would be upset if you had been pestered as I am. People asking, "Where are the geese?" and "Who did you sell the geese to?" I'm sick of it.'

Holmes smiled. 'Well, I have nothing to do with any of those people. But I have a bet on that those geese were country-bred geese.'

The man looked sideways at Holmes. 'Well, you will lose your money,' he said. 'They are town-bred.'

'It cannot be,' said Holmes. 'You cannot fool me about such birds.'

'Do you think you know more about them than I do? I have handled fowls since I was a nipper!'

34

'Nonsense,' said Holmes. 'You are confused, that's all.'

'Will you bet with me then?' asked the man.

'I'll put a sovereign on it,' said Holmes. 'But how can you prove it?'

The man chuckled. 'Bring me the books, Bill!'

A small boy brought a thin black book. The man opened it. 'Now, Mr Know-All, let us see. Here we have all the records of what is bought and sold.' He ran his finger down the page. 'Perhaps you would read what it says there, sir?' He pointed at an entry in the book.

'Mrs Oakshott, 117 Brixton Road,' read Holmes.

'And on the page facing?' said the man with a smile.

'December 22nd. Twenty-four geese at seven shillings and sixpence.'

'And next to that?'

'Sold to Mr Windigate of the Alpha, at twelve shillings.'

'What have you to say now?' asked the man with a smile of triumph.

Holmes shook his head and pulled a sovereign from his pocket. He turned away as if he was too disappointed to speak. We had walked a few yards when he stopped and winked at me. 'I know a betting man when I see one,' he said.

'And are we going to Brixton Road now?' I asked. It was getting late and very cold. I knew, however, that if Holmes was on the trail, nothing would stop him.

Holmes was about to answer when there was a noise from the stall. Breckinridge was waving his arms in the air and shouting at a small man with a sharp, pointed face.

'If you come pestering me any more, I will set the dog on you! You bring Mrs Oakshott here and I'll answer her. What have you to do with it? Did I buy the geese off you?'

'No, but one of them was mine all the same,' the man whined.

'Well, ask Mrs Oakshott for it.'

'She told me to ask you.'

'Well, you can ask the King of Russia for it for all I care. Get out of here!'

'This may save us a trip to Brixton Road,' said Holmes. 'Let us see what we can make of this fellow.' He hurried after the man who had asked the questions.

'Excuse me,' said Holmes. 'I heard you asking the salesman about geese. I think I may be able to help you.'

'How can you know anything about it?' the man said suspiciously.

'My name is Sherlock Holmes and it is my business to know what other people do not know. You are trying to track down some geese sold by Mrs Oakshott. Those geese were sold to Mr Windigate of the Alpha Inn. Mr Henry Baker is a member of that goose club.'

The man stretched out his hand. 'You are the man I have longed to meet,' he said.

'Indeed,' said Holmes. 'Then we had better discuss it in a warm room, not here in the street.' He stopped a cab and we all got in. 'May I know your name?'

'Er, John Robinson,' said the man with a sideways glance.

'No, no,' said Holmes sweetly, 'your *real* name. It is always hard doing business with an alias.'

The man's white face went red for a moment. 'James Ryder,' he said.

'Exactly,' said Holmes. 'Porter at the Cosmopolitan Hotel, I believe?'

Nothing more was said during the journey to Baker Street. Ryder looked as if he did not know what to make of things. Was this a stroke of good luck or bad?

CHAPTER 4

The Game is Up

We entered Holmes' study where the fire was still burning. Mrs Hudson, Holmes' housekeeper, had clearly been looking after it.

'You look cold,' said Holmes. 'Do sit near the fire. Now, you want to know what became of those geese?'

'Yes, sir.'

'Or one special goose. Perhaps a goose with a black bar across the tail?'

Ryder's eyes opened wide. 'Can you tell me where it went to?'

'It came here.'

'Here?'

'Yes. And a very special bird it was. Do you know, it laid an egg after it was dead! A bright blue egg.' Holmes opened his strong box and took out the blue carbuncle, which shone like a star.

Ryder stood up. I thought he might fall over but he held on to the table. He stared at the jewel.

'The game's up, Ryder,' said Holmes. He turned to me. 'Give him a dash of brandy. He hasn't the blood for this sort of crime.'

The brandy brought some colour back to the man's cheeks. He sat staring at Holmes with his eyes full of fear.

'I know enough to put you behind bars,' said Holmes coldly. 'You may as well tell me the rest. You had heard of this jewel belonging to the Countess of Morcar?'

'It was Catherine Cusack who told me. The lady's maid.'

'I see. Not a pretty crime, Ryder. You were happy that

Horner should go to prison for it. You knew he had a prison record so you asked him to come and repair the fire in the Countess's room. You probably caused the damage yourself and he walked into your little trap. The trap set by you and Catherine Cusack!'

Ryder fell on the rug and begged at Holmes' feet. 'Have mercy!' he cried. 'Think of my father. Think of my mother. It would break their hearts. I never went wrong before. I never will again!'

'Get back in your chair,' said Holmes sternly. 'It is all very well to whine now and beg now but you thought little enough of this poor Horner who stands accused!'

'I will go away. I will leave the country. Without me, the case against him will not stand up.'

Holmes was silent. Then he said, 'We shall see. Tell me the true story of how the jewel got into the goose. Tell me the truth, for it is your only hope.'

'After Horner was arrested, I knew I had to hide the jewel. The police would search the hotel. So I went to my sister's house in Brixton Road. While we stood in the yard where the geese were, I was thinking how I could get the stone to someone I knew over in Kilburn, someone who might be able to get money for it.

'My sister had said I could have a goose for Christmas. As I looked at them I had the idea that would save me. No one would look for the jewel in a goose!

'When my sister went inside I caught one of the birds,

one with a black barred tail. I prized its bill open and pushed the jewel down it. It gave a gulp and the jewel passed down the gullet into the crop.

'Just then my sister came out again. I let go of the bird and asked her if I could have my goose for Christmas. "Of course," she said. "Take your pick." So I caught the one with the barred tail, killed it and took it to Kilburn.

'But when we opened up the crop we found nothing! My heart turned to water. I left it there and rushed back to my sister. The yard was empty! All the birds had gone. She told me they had all gone to the dealer in Covent Garden. "Was there another one with a barred tail?" I asked. "Yes," she said, "there were two barred-tailed ones. I never could tell them apart.'' And that man would never tell me where he had sold them.

'I tried again tonight. You heard me. My sister thinks I am mad. I think I am going mad. Now I am a thief and I have never had any gains from my crime. God help me!' He burst into sobs, his face in his hands.

There was a long silence. At last Holmes got up and went to the door. 'Get out!' he said, opening it.

'Oh, sir. Heaven bless you!'

'No more words. Be gone.'

No more words were needed. Holmes turned to me, reaching out his hand for his clay pipe, and said, 'I am not here to make up for what the police lack. If Ryder is sent to jail he'll be in and out of prison all his life. He won't go wrong again – he's had too much of a fright. Nor will he go to court against Horner. The case will collapse.' He stretched out his long legs towards the fire. 'Just think, Watson, we began with a hat and a goose! Chance placed in our way a most odd problem – and I think its solution is its own reward.'

The Adventure of Silver Blaze

CHAPTER I

A Disappearance and a Death

'I am afraid, Watson, that I shall have to go,' said Holmes, looking up from his newspaper.

'Go? Where to?' I asked.

'To Dartmoor. To King's Pyland.'

I was not surprised. The disappearance of the horse called Silver Blaze was a big story, covered in all the newspapers. Silver Blaze was the favourite to win the Wessex Cup but the horse was now missing and its trainer had been murdered.

'I would be happy to go with you,' I said. 'As long as I'm not in the way.'

'My dear Watson, you would do me a great favour. This looks like a unique case.'

And so it happened that an hour or so later we were on our way to King's Pyland, home of the famous stables. On the way, Holmes told me the details of the case.

'Silver Blaze has won many prizes for his owner, Colonel Ross. He was also the favourite to win the Wessex

Cup. The horse is well liked by the public and a lot of money has been staked on him. It is clear, then, that many people had a strong interest in preventing Silver Blaze from starting.'

'What about the trainer?'

'John Straker had been the trainer for seven years, and had a clean record. There were three stable lads. One of them sat up each night in the stable while the others slept up in the loft. According to my information, they are all reliable servants.'

'Do we know anything more about Straker?' I asked.

'He was a married man without children, who lived in a small house near the stables. The country around is very lonely but about half a mile north there is a group of houses. Across the moor, about two miles, are the Mapleton stables. They are owned by Lord Blackwater and managed by Silas Brown. In all other directions the moor is deserted apart from a few gypsies who roam the area.'

'Tell me more,' I said.

'On the evening in question the horses were fed and watered as usual and the stables were locked at nine o'clock. Two of the lads went up to the trainer's house where they had supper. The other lad, Ned Hunter, was left on guard. Shortly after nine, the maid, Edith, took Ned his supper, a dish of curried mutton.'

'No drink?'

'There was a tap in the stable. It was a rule that the lad on duty must drink nothing else. Edith was a little way from the stables when she was stopped by a man. She said he was "a gentleman" and wore a grey suit and a cloth cap. He carried a heavy stick and she noticed that his face was very pale and that he seemed nervous.'

'Go on, Holmes. I have not heard any of this so far.'

'As ever, the newspapers only have room for *some* of the facts,' said Holmes. 'The man said to Edith, "Can you tell me where I am?" She told him he was close to King's Pyland stables. "What a stroke of luck," he said. "Now, I am sure you would like to earn the price of a new dress," and he tried to give her a piece of paper to give to the stable boy.

'But Edith ran to the stable where Ned was already at the little table by the window. He looked up and she passed him his meal as normal. As she started to tell him what had happened, the stranger appeared again. "Good evening," he said to Ned, through the open window. "I wanted to have a word with you."

'"What do you want here?" asked the lad.

'"Just some information — which I will pay you for. Tell me, is it true that the horse Bayard could beat the other horses hands down, even if they had five furlongs' start — and that the stables have put their money on him?"

' "We don't talk about that sort of thing to people like you!" said the lad. "And we don't want your sort round here!" He got up to set the dog free. The girl ran off but she saw the stranger still leaning through the window. Yet when Ned came out of the stable with the dog, the man had gone.'

'Did the stable boy leave the door unlocked behind him?'

'Excellent, Watson,' murmured Holmes. 'I asked the same question. I was told that Ned locked the door.'

'And the window?'

'Not big enough for a man to get through. Ned waited

till the other lads came back and then he sent a message to the trainer. Straker was uneasy when he heard what had happened. At one o'clock his wife woke up to find him dressing. He said he was going to see that all was well.'

'That was the last she saw of him?'

'The last she saw of him alive. At seven o'clock she woke and went down to the stables. She saw Ned Hunter fast asleep – or drunk. The horse was missing and there was no sign of the trainer.

'She woke the lads in the loft but they had heard nothing. Ned, however, could not be roused and so they left him to sleep. The lads and the woman ran off to search.

'A short way off they found the body of the trainer.

He had a dreadful head wound and a long cut in the thigh. He seemed to have put up a fight; his hand still held a small knife which had blood on it up to the handle. In his left hand he held a red and black silk cravat, which the maid said she had seen the stranger wearing. When Ned recovered from his drugged sleep he also recognized the cravat.'

'And what of the horse?'

'There were signs that the horse had been at the scene of the murder. However, it has since been impossible to find it.'

'How was the lad drugged?'

'Traces of powdered opium were found in the remains of his supper.'

I whistled. 'And what of the stranger? Has he been found?'

'He has been found – and arrested by Inspector Gregory, who is in charge of the case. His name is Fitzroy Simpson and he lived in one of the nearby houses. He has lost a fortune betting on horses and he now lives by placing bets for others and giving racing tips. Bets of five thousand pounds had been laid by him against the favourite, Silver Blaze.'

'Damning evidence, wouldn't you say? What was his story?'

'He admitted coming to get information about the horses at King's Pyland. He also wanted to find out about the horses at the other stables, at Mapleton. That is where the second favourite, Desborough, is to be found. He did not deny being at the stables but said he had no other plans.'

'But what about the cravat?'

'Indeed. He could not explain how it came to be in the hand of the dead man. He also still had his stick, which could have been the weapon that killed Straker.'

'Then there is no mystery?'

'There were no wounds on his person – and Straker's knife shows that someone must have been injured.'

'Perhaps the blood on the knife is Straker's own?'

'That is quite possible. The police believe that Simpson drugged the lad and kidnapped the horse. Perhaps Simpson had a copy of the key from somewhere. Silver Blaze's bridle is missing, so he must have put it on. Somewhere, the police think, he met the trainer and a fight took place.'

'And the horse bolted?' I suggested.

'Or was taken to a hiding place. Though how Simpson expected to get away with such a crime is, indeed, a mystery.' At this point Holmes sank back into thought and remained so for the rest of the journey.

CHAPTER 2

On the Trail

When we arrived at the station, we met Colonel Ross and Inspector Gregory. They helped us into their carriage and we set off for King's Pyland.

'Thank you for coming, Mr Holmes,' said the Colonel. 'I am determined to avenge poor Straker – and to recover my horse.'

'The evidence against Simpson is very strong,' said the Inspector calmly. 'He had much to gain if Silver Blaze could not race. Things like the stick and the cravat are very much against him.'

Holmes shook his head. 'A clever defence lawyer would tear it to shreds,' he said. 'Why take the horse out

of the stable? He could injure it where it was. Has a copy of the key been found? Where did he get the opium? Above all, where would he hide a horse?'

The Inspector nodded. He did not resent Holmes' objections and he took a while to reply. 'A key could be thrown away on the moors. He could obtain opium in London, where he came from. And the horse may very well be at the bottom of one of the many pits or mines in the area.'

'What does he say about the cravat?'

'He admits it was his and says that he lost it. There is one other clue, however.'

'Yes?' asked Holmes.

'A party of gypsies were camped within a mile of the spot where Straker was found. The following day they had gone. Simpson may have passed the horse on to them. We are searching for them now.'

'And the other stables? The Mapleton stables?'

'We have been there. The trainer at Mapleton, Silas Brown, certainly had large bets on the race; and he was no friend of poor Straker. But there is nothing to connect him with the affair.'

'And nothing to connect this man Simpson with the interests of the Mapleton stables?'

'Nothing at all.'

Holmes leaned back in the carriage and the conversation ceased.

When we stepped out of the carriage, I noticed that Holmes had a gleam in his eye. I knew he had already thought of something that the others had missed.

'I should like to see what Straker had with him at the time of his death,' he said.

The Inspector nodded amiably and led him into the front room of the house. On the table was a small heap of things: a box of matches, a piece of candle, a pipe, a tobacco pouch, a silver watch with a gold chain, five sovereigns, a pencil case, a few papers and an ivory-handled knife with a blade marked 'Weiss & Co'. It was still stained with blood.

'This is a very special knife,' said Holmes. 'This is in your line, Watson.'

'Yes,' I said. 'It is what we call a cataract knife. A very delicate blade for very delicate work.'

'A strange thing for a man to carry on a rough night, especially as it would not close in his pocket.'

'His wife told us it was on the dressing table before he went out,' said the Inspector. 'It had a cork to guard the tip. Perhaps it was the best weapon he could think of as he left the house.'

'The papers are of interest,' said Holmes, turning over a pile of documents with his long fingers. 'In particular this bill from a dress shop for thirty-seven pounds, made out to William Darbyshire. This Darbyshire was a friend of Straker's, according to his wife.'

'Someone has expensive tastes,' I smiled.

As we left, a woman, pale and haggard, stopped us. 'What have you found?' she asked. Holmes did not answer her directly. Smiling gently, he said, 'Surely we have met?'

The woman shook her head.

'You were dressed in dove-coloured silk with ostrich feather trimming?'

'You are mistaken. I never had such a dress,' said the woman.

Holmes apologized and followed the Inspector outside.

A short walk took us to the murder spot where Holmes bent to examine the ground. He took a long time and the Colonel became impatient, often looking at his watch while Holmes continued his systematic search.

'Ah-ha!' Holmes said at last, and picked out a half-burnt match. He then took some time comparing the prints in the mud with a boot of John Straker's and one of Silver Blaze's horseshoes. Finally he turned back to the Colonel. 'Now, if you will excuse us, Watson and I will take a walk a little over the moors. I shall put the horseshoe in my pocket for luck.'

As we walked away, in the direction of Mapleton, he said, 'Where is the horse? It is a puzzle. Let us imagine what might happen to it. Would it run loose for long? No. Horses seek company. Kidnapped by gypsies? They would never be able to sell a horse like that. A loose horse would make for Mapleton or King's Pyland. It is not at King's Pyland. Therefore it must be at Mapleton.'

We soon came to a dip in the land where Holmes stopped. 'This must have been wet on Monday night. Let us see if there are tracks here.'

He soon gave a shout. I ran over and found him fitting the horseshoe into the mark in the mud. 'Such is the value of imagination, Watson. It is the one thing Inspector Gregory lacks.'

As we got closer to Mapleton, we saw the marks of the horse once more, this time with a man's tracks beside them. Suddenly they changed direction again, towards King's Pyland. Holmes whistled. Then I spotted the same tracks, returning towards Mapleton.

'Well done,' said Holmes. 'You have saved us a walk.'

As we came near to the gates of Mapleton stables, a groom ran out and asked what we wanted.

'If I called at five o'clock tomorrow morning to see your master, Silas Brown, would I be too early?' enquired Holmes genially.

'No, sir. He is always the first up and about. But here he comes now!'

A cross-looking gentleman came through the gate. 'What the devil do you want here?'

'Ten minutes of your time,' said Holmes calmly.

'I've no time for gossiping,' said the man. He turned as if to go, but Holmes stepped forward, laid a hand on his arm, and whispered in his ear. Immediately Brown's face reddened with fury. 'It's a lie!' he cried. 'An infernal lie!'

'Very well,' said Holmes. 'Shall we argue about it in public or indoors?'

'Oh, come in, if you must,' said the man.

CHAPTER 3

A Horse is Found

I waited for twenty minutes. At last, Holmes and the trainer came out. Silas Brown's face was no longer red but grey. His hands were shaking and he was covered in sweat. 'It will be done as you say,' was all he said.

'There must be no mistake.' There was menace in Holmes' voice.

'You can trust me,' said the man.

'You will hear from me tomorrow.' And Holmes walked away.

After a little distance, he said, 'What a coward and a bully. He tried to deny it but I described so exactly what had happened that he thought I had seen him. You may have noticed that his boots fitted the tracks by the side of the horse's . . . '

'What did you describe to him?' I asked, amazed.

'I said that early in the morning, he saw a strange horse wandering nearby. When he got closer he realized it was Silver Blaze. He started to lead it back to King's Pyland – but then he saw a better plan. If he hid Silver Blaze till after the race, his horse would almost certainly win!'

'But the stables have been searched,' I said.

'An old horse-faker like him has many a trick.'

'And now?'

'We return to London.'

'To London? But what of Straker's killer?'

'All in good time, Watson. We have business in town.' And Holmes would say no more.

The Colonel gave a sneer when Holmes told him he was leaving. 'So we are no further forward than when you arrived?' I could see that he was not impressed with my friend's achievements.

'We shall see,' said Holmes. 'But you have my word that your horse will run in the Wessex Cup.'

'I would rather have my horse than your word,' said the Colonel.

Holmes looked at him coldly.

As we left, Holmes spoke to one of the stable lads. 'You have a few sheep here. Who looks after them?'

'I do, sir.'

'Anything wrong with them lately?'

'Well, three have gone lame.'

Holmes grinned and rubbed his hands together. 'A long shot, Watson! Remember that point, Inspector.'

'Anything else?' asked Inspector Gregory, looking interested.

'Yes, the strange incident of the dog in the night.'

'But the dog did nothing.'

'That was the strange incident,' said Holmes.

CHAPTER 4

The Wessex Cup

Four days later, Holmes and I set off for Winchester, to see the Wessex Cup. Colonel Ross met us at the racecourse. His face was grave and his manner was cold.

'I have seen nothing of my horse,' said he.

'You would know him?' asked Holmes, with a smile.

'Of course!' said Ross angrily. 'With the white blaze on his head and the white mark on his foreleg! Do you take me for a fool?'

Holmes did not reply. He looked at the betting. 'I see Silver Blaze is still favourite,' was all he would say.

'There are six in the race,' I said, 'and all six numbers are up. There must be six horses entered.'

'But I don't see him!' cried the Colonel.

'Let us see how they run,' replied Holmes with a confident smile.

To begin with, the horses were all close together. Then Desborough, the Mapleton horse, took the lead. However, two furlongs from the winning post, a big bay horse swept into the lead and won easily by six lengths.

'Let us go to the winners' enclosure,' said Holmes and led the way.

Once inside, he turned to the Colonel. 'Here is your horse. Just wash his face and his leg in spirit and you will recognize Silver Blaze.'

'My horse! But how – ?'

'I found him in the hands of a gentleman who is well-versed in such things. To him it was an easy matter to hide Silver Blaze's white markings. He was put in the race just as he looked when he arrived.'

The Colonel shook his head. 'You have done wonders and I owe you an apology. You have found my horse. If only you could find the killer of John Straker.'

'I have done so. He is here,' said Holmes.

For a moment the Colonel looked angry again. Then

Holmes said, 'The murderer is behind you.' He put his hand on the neck of the horse. 'It was self-defence!'

CHAPTER 5

Holmes Explains

Later Holmes explained. 'It was the curried mutton, the only dish which would hide the taste of opium. Yet how could Simpson have known that Ned's food that night would be curry? It was impossible. So my suspicion fell on Straker and his wife. They were the only ones who could decide on the food.'

He continued, 'Then there was the dog. The dog that did not bark when a stranger came in the night! The sleeping stable lads in the loft would have heard it bark – but it was silent. It would only be silent if it knew the person who came in.'

'But why would Straker want to steal his own horse?' I asked, still mystified.

'To injure it so that it could not race, because he had money on the second favourite. But it had to be done in a way which would not be noticed. Remember the knife designed for delicate operations? Straker planned to use it to nick the tendons of the horse's leg. A small nick would not be seen but would make the horse lame.'

'Scoundrel!' cried the Colonel.

'Straker had to do this somewhere quiet so he took the horse onto the moors. He needed the candle in order to see what he was doing – '

' – And you found the match!' I said. 'But what drove him to this?'

'A woman, my dear Watson. You remember the bill? Men do not carry other people's bills. Straker was also known as Darbyshire.'

'And he was buying expensive dresses for another woman?'

'That was easy to discover. You may remember that I found out from Mrs Straker that she had never had such a dress. The shop's address was on the bill. So we returned to London and they recognized the photograph of Straker.'

'But what of the cravat?'

'Simpson dropped it in his hurry to get away. Straker saw it and maybe hoped it would be useful in tying the horse's leg. He took the horse to the hollow and tried to carry out his plan but he had not reckoned on the horse. It lashed out and its hoof struck Straker on the head. He fell and the knife cut his leg.'

'What about the sheep?' I asked, remembering Holmes' enquiry of the lad.

'That was a long shot! I thought a man like Straker would take care to practise – and where better than on a sheep or two?'

'And all to make money on Silas Brown's horse!' cried the Colonel.

'Desperate actions of a desperate man,' said Holmes.

'But where *was* the horse?' asked the Colonel.

'Ahem,' said Holmes. 'It bolted...and was looked after by a horse-lover, shall we say. Perhaps the less said about that, the better. Shall we go and place a bet on the last race of the day?'

The Adventure of the Copper Beeches

CHAPTER I

A Dangerous Offer

It was a cold morning in early spring. Holmes and I were sitting each side of a cheery fire in the old room in Baker Street. Holmes was not in a good mood and puffed irritably on his pipe. 'Crime is common. Logic is rare,' he said, 'and who cares for logic any more? My work seems to be nothing more than an agency for recovering lost pencils and giving advice to young ladies from boarding schools.'

I stayed silent. Holmes was best left alone in this mood.

'This note,' he continued, 'marks the lowest point of my career. Read it!'

He tossed a crumpled letter to me. It said:

Dear Mr Holmes

I am very anxious to consult you as to whether I should or should not accept a post as governess. I shall call at half past ten tomorrow if that is convenient to you.

Yours faithfully,

Violet Hunter.

At that moment the bell rang and shortly after, a young woman, plainly but neatly dressed, entered the room. She had a bright face and a brisk, businesslike manner.

'I am sorry to trouble you,' she said, 'but I have had a very strange experience. I have no parents or anyone else to ask for advice.'

'Do take a seat, Miss Hunter,' said Holmes. 'I shall be happy to help you if I can.'

Miss Hunter began: 'I have been a governess for five years. Two months ago my employer went to Canada and I found myself without a job. I use an agency in London called Westaways, which is managed by a Miss Stoper. I call once a week to see if there's a job to suit me. You will understand that I have very few savings and I need to find a post very soon.

'Last week when I called, Miss Stoper was not alone in her office. There was a man with her – a very stout man with a smiling, ruddy face.

'When I came in he said, "That will do! I could not ask for better!" Then he spoke to me with a most engaging smile. "What salary do you ask?"

' "Four pounds a month."

' "Pitiful!" he cried. "Your salary with me would start at a hundred pounds a year."

'This seemed too good to be true. I felt that I needed to know more so I asked, "May I enquire where you live, sir?"

'"Hampshire. A place called Copper Beeches near Winchester."

'"And what would my duties be?"

'"One child of six, that's all. You should see him killing cockroaches with a slipper! Smack, smack, smack!"

'"My only duties are to look after the one child?" I asked, wanting to be sure.

'"Your duty would be to obey any little commands which my wife might give. Nothing out of the ordinary, I assure you."

'"I should be happy to make myself useful."

'"Quite so. Now . . . about the matter of dress. We are faddy people – but kind. If we asked you to wear a special dress, for example, would you object?"

'"No," I said, though I was surprised.

'"And to cut your hair short?"

'I could hardly believe my ears. My hair is my pride and joy.

'"Oh," I said, without thinking what I was saying, "I'm afraid that is impossible."

'"But it must be done," said the man. "My wife has these fancies and you know how such fancies must be obeyed . . ."

'"I'm sorry," I said. "It really is impossible."

'His smile disappeared; he looked disappointed. "What a shame. In all other ways you are quite perfect."

'Miss Stoper looked upset and cross. As I left the

room I thought that I would now be unlikely to get a job through her agency. When I got home and saw more bills to be paid, I thought I had been foolish. I had lost a good job just by refusing to cut my hair!

'The next day, however, there was a letter from the man, who was called Jephro Rucastle. He offered to raise the salary to £120 a year and asked me again to take the post.'

She passed the letter to Sherlock Holmes. He read it with interest.

'Should I take the job, Mr Holmes?'

Holmes sighed. 'I think your mind is already made up.'

'Should I refuse? I do need the money and the salary is good.'

'It is too good. Why should he pay £120 when he could get someone for £40? I would not like a sister of mine to take such a job.'

She looked downcast. 'I thought if I told you all about it – I might be able to ask your help if I needed it.'

'You may rely on my support. If you find yourself in danger – '

'Danger!' she cried. 'What danger do you foresee?'

'It would cease to be a danger if we knew what it was. Send me a telegram any time, day or night, and we shall be there.'

Violet stood up. 'Thank you. I shall go down to Copper Beeches easy in my mind. Tonight I shall cut my hair and tomorrow I shall travel to Winchester.' She thanked us and left.

'We will hear from her before many days have passed,' said Holmes. He sighed – but he already seemed to be more cheerful.

CHAPTER 2

A Telegram Arrives

Holmes' words turned out to be correct. A fortnight later a telegram came.

Please be at the Black Swan Hotel in Winchester at midday tomorrow. Do come. I am at my wit's end. Hunter.

By eleven o'clock the next day we were on our way.

'The countryside seems a peaceful place,' said Holmes, as he looked out of the train window. 'But think what can go on in the deserted houses and hamlets. In the country, there is no one to report the evil which may be taking place.'

His words were chilling and I was glad to see Violet Hunter safe at the Black Swan when we arrived.

'I am so delighted that you have come,' she said, earnestly.

We sat in a quiet corner. 'Let us have everything in its due order,' said Holmes, thrusting his long thin legs out towards the fire and closing his eyes to listen.

Violet began her story.

CHAPTER 3

Violet's Story

I have had no ill-treatment but I cannot understand Mr and Mrs Rucastle. I must say I am not easy in my mind about them.

When I came here, Mr Rucastle met me and drove me to the house. It is in a very nice spot but the house itself is not beautiful. It was once white but is now badly stained and streaked by damp and bad weather. In front of the house are the copper beeches which give it its name.

Mrs Rucastle is a silent, pale-faced woman, much younger than her husband. He is a widower and already has a grown-up daughter who, I was told, had gone to America. Mr Rucastle married again and now has a son of six: a spoilt, ill-natured boy who seems to enjoy giving pain to anything weaker than himself.

Then there are the servants, Mr and Mrs Toller. Mr Toller is a rough, uncouth man with grizzled hair and whiskers. He always smells of drink and I have twice seen him completely drunk, though Mr Rucastle seems to take no notice.

Mrs Toller is tall and strong. She has a sour face and

is as silent as Mrs Rucastle. They are a very unpleasant couple.

The first day I was there, Mr Rucastle took me to an outhouse and showed me a huge animal. 'This is Carlo, my hound,' he said. 'Toller is the only one who can control him. We let him loose at night. Do not ever set foot outside at night! It is as much as your life is worth!'

The sight of that dreadful animal sent a chill to my heart.

On the third day Mr Rucastle called me to his study. 'Thank you for pleasing us by cutting your hair,' he said. 'I wonder if you would put on the dress which is on your bed, then come to the drawing-room.'

The dress which I found in my room was an unusual blue. It had been worn before but it fitted me very well. When I entered the drawing-room, Mr and Mrs Rucastle were very pleased and said how much it suited me.

They asked me to sit close to the long windows, which I did. The chair faced away from the window, so I could not see out. Mr Rucastle walked up and down telling me stories. He was a good teller of very funny stories and I laughed a lot, but Mrs Rucastle just sat and looked sad.

Two days later I was asked to do the same thing. Again I changed my dress and again I sat in the window. Once more Mr Rucastle told me stories.

I was very curious and wanted to see what was going on behind my back. The next time I hid my small hand mirror in my handkerchief. I pretended I was wiping my eyes from laughing so much but, using it, I managed to see out onto the road. There was a man looking up at the window.

I think Mrs Rucastle saw what I was doing. She stood up. 'Jephro,' she said, 'there is a man on the road staring at Miss Hunter.'

'Dear me. How rude of him. Please, Miss Hunter, turn round and wave him away.'

I did as I was told. Mr Rucastle then drew down the blind. I was not asked to sit near the window again, nor was I asked to wear the blue dress any more.

After a few days I had a good idea of the layout of the house. There was one wing where no one seemed to live. The door to that part of the house was always locked.

When I looked at that wing from outside I saw that there were four windows in a row. Three of them looked dirty but the other one had shutters which were closed.

When I asked Mr Rucastle about it, he looked startled. 'Photography is one of my hobbies,' he said. 'I have a dark-room there. What a clever young lady to notice such things.' He spoke in a joking tone but I think he was annoyed.

I was very curious and I also had a feeling that I ought to find out more. Yesterday my chance came. Toller was very drunk. He had left a key in the door to the hidden part of the house so I was able to open the door and slip through.

In front of me was a little passage, off which I could see several doors. They were all open except one, under which there was a light showing. It was fastened with a huge padlock. I stood gazing at the sinister door and wondering what was behind it. Then there was a sound of steps inside the room. Suddenly I felt very scared and I turned and ran back down the passage, clutching at the skirt of my dress.

As I rushed through the door, I ran straight into Mr Rucastle.

'So!' he said. 'What have you been up to?'

'Oh, I am so frightened,' I cried.

'What has frightened you?' he asked quietly. His voice was coaxing – but I was careful what I said.

'I was foolish enough to go into the empty wing. But it is so lonely and still in there, I suddenly felt scared.'

He looked at me and his eyes became hard and fierce. 'Now you know why I keep it locked and if I find you there again . . . I shall throw you to the hound!'

CHAPTER 4

The Rescue

'I ran to my room,' Violet continued. 'Everything seemed horrible: the house, the servants, the Rucastles – even the child. I used my afternoon off to walk into the village and send the telegram. This morning I slipped out of the house while the Rucastles were out. Toller was completely drunk and Mrs Toller was in the kitchen garden.' She paused and looked at Holmes. 'I am so glad to see you here. I know there is something wrong but I cannot work out what it can be.'

'We shall soon unravel this,' Holmes said, rising and pacing up and down the room. 'Is there a cellar with a strong lock?'

'Why, yes,' she said, 'the wine cellar.'

'You have been a brave and sensible girl. Can you do one more thing before we arrive?'

'I will try.'

'Get Mrs Toller to go to the cellar for some reason. Close and lock the door.'

'I will do it!'

'Excellent. You are a quite exceptional woman. We shall follow in forty minutes. The only explanation is that you have been brought to Copper Beeches to impersonate someone. That person must be the daughter, Alice Rucastle. I fear that she is locked in the room which you discovered.'

'How dreadful! But why?' asked Violet.

'The man in the road – the one you saw – must be her sweetheart, perhaps her fiancé. You were brought there to show that Alice was alive and happy. You even waved him away, which they hoped would be enough to convince him that you no longer wished to see him.'

'But, I ask again, why go to such extremes?'

'That,' said Holmes, 'is what we shall find out.'

Forty minutes later we arrived at Copper Beeches. Violet Hunter was waiting on the steps as we approached. 'Have you managed it?' asked Holmes.

A loud thudding came from somewhere downstairs. 'It is Mrs Toller in the cellar,' Violet said. 'Her husband is snoring on the kitchen rug. Here are his keys.'

'You have done well indeed!' cried Holmes with enthusiasm. 'Now lead us to the room.'

We went up the stairs, unlocked the door and walked

down the passage. We came to the padlocked door. 'Try your shoulder against it, Watson,' said Holmes.

The door gave way easily and together we entered the room. It was empty. All we saw was a simple bed, a small table and a basket of clothes.

'Look!' said Violet.

Above, in the ceiling, was a skylight. It was open. The prisoner was gone.

With my help, Holmes made his way up through the skylight. 'Yes,' he called, 'there is a ladder over there.' He dropped back into the room. 'Someone is coming,' he whispered. 'Watson, have your pistol ready.'

A fat, burly man appeared in the doorway with a heavy stick in his hand. Violet screamed and held on to my arm. Holmes strode up to him. 'You villain. Where is your daughter?'

Rucastle's eyes were wide. He looked round and then saw the open skylight. 'It is for you to tell me that! You thieves! Just wait!' He ran off down the passage.

'He's gone for the hound!' cried Violet.

'I have my revolver,' I said.

We rushed along the passage and down the stairs. We reached the hall. Suddenly we heard a dreadful barking noise. Then there was a scream of agony. An old man with a red face and shaking limbs staggered into the room. It was Toller.

'My God!' he cried. 'Someone has loosed the dog. It has not been fed for two days. Quick, or it will be too late!'

We rushed out and round the side of the house. There we saw the huge hungry brute, its black muzzle buried in Rucastle's throat. The man writhed and screamed on the ground. Pistol in hand, I ran closer and blew out its brains. As it fell over its teeth were still locked onto the flesh of Rucastle's neck.

The facts of the case were finally put together from Toller and his wife. Holmes explained on the train back to London.

'Alice Rucastle had money of her own but was happy to let her father handle her affairs. All was well until Alice fell in love with a naval officer. Rucastle knew that if she married, he would lose Alice's money.'

'So he locked her in the east wing and employed Violet to get rid of him?'

'Exactly. An extreme plan – but Rucastle is an extreme man, with a cruel temper like his son. But the seaman did not go away. He too worked out what was going on. He bribed Mrs Toller and gave old Mr Toller as much rum as he could drink. Then he brought the ladder and – '

'Rescued the maiden. Just like in the fairy tale.'

'Exactly, Watson. And it was good to be on hand when Rucastle returned. Who can tell what he would have done to Miss Hunter when he found that Alice had gone!'

Rucastle lived but he was from then on a sick man, kept alive by his devoted, sad wife. Alice Rucastle and her sailor were married. Violet Hunter is now the head of a school in Walsall, where I believe she has made a most successful career.